THE G.O.O.D. MONEY MANUAL

THE G.O.O.D. MONEY MANUAL

A STUDENT'S GUIDE TO AVOID LIVING PAYCHECK TO PAYCHECK

by

Darryl Boyles

The G.O.O.D. Money Manual:
Darryl Boyles

First Edition, 2023

TABLE OF CONTENTS

INTRODUCTION 1

CHAPTER 1
ENVIRONMENT 3

CHAPTER 2
INCOME 8

CHAPTER 3
DEBT 12

CHAPTER 4
CREDIT 31

CHAPTER 5
SAVINGS 41

CHAPTER 6
INVESTING 101 48

CHAPTER 7
STOCK MARKET 101 60

CHAPTER 8
EMPOWERMENT 66

WHAT YOU'LL LEARN IN EACH CHAPTER

Introduction:
Who I am and why I'm here to help.

Chapter 1: Environment
Different people, similar struggles.

Chapter 2: Income
Different ways of making and planning money.

Chapter 3: Debt
Learn about the biggest contributors of how you can avoid them.

Chapter 4: Credit
Learn the ins and outs of credit and how you can establish good scores.

Chapter 5: Savings
Learn about different ways to be strategic in order to build your savings.

Chapter 6: Investing 101
Learn how to lay the foundation to have your money doing your hard work.

Chapter 7: Stocks 101
Learn about the different ways to become part owner of some of the best publicly traded companies.

Chapter 8: Empowerment
My Challenge to You.

INTRODUCTION

When I first made the commitment to myself to learn more about finances for the sake of improving my own, I noticed that a lot of the financial gurus were talking to people who already had money. People who had access to borrow money with good credit, retirement plans, owned homes, and received inherences from loved ones who passed away. Myself, and the majority of people I grew up around, didn't share this same story. Therefore, the financial information they were giving wouldn't apply in the same way because I wasn't, nor were the people I knew, in their position.

I didn't need information on how to diversify my portfolio: I needed some information to help me get out of living paycheck-to-paycheck. As I travel and present financial literacy workshops to various schools and organizations, I always keep this in mind. My goal is to help empower the everyday person, and I know that they don't come from a perfect financial situation. I also know that they don't have many people to turn to financially for help, if anybody at all. The responsibility of preventing or exiting a paycheck-to-paycheck lifestyle will be squarely on their own shoulders.

The everyday person didn't grow up learning about investing and having their money work for them. Instead, they were taught to make more money by putting in more hours on the job, which is a necessary step in the process of improving finances for most people. But, not hiring your money to work for you is a decision that leads to financial frustration. This is why the majority of working adults are living paycheck-to-paycheck. I, like so many others, lacked the financial information needed to lay the foundation of having my money work for me. The information I will share in this book comes from years of struggling and years of studying. And, although I wrote this book for teenage students, the information can be applied to adults as well. So, whether you are in school or have teenage kids who are in school, the information in this book can help you with your finances.

I'm a certified financial education instructor, certified credit specialist, certified public speaker, and a 3-time author, but my best education comes from growing up in situations similar to my audiences. This is one of the main reasons I connect with my audience so well: I speak their language, I've lived similar struggles, and my heart's desire is to see them improve their circumstances. I've lived paycheck-to-paycheck enough to understand how struggling financially has the ability to affect every aspect of your life. Many of life's decisions are based on what we can afford, not what we desire, and when your money is limited so are your options.

It's a horrible feeling to be a full time working adult while still being at the mercy of someone else because of your finances. Money equals power in today's society, and the purpose of this book is to educate and empower you to avoid the consequences of living paycheck-to-paycheck. This book seeks to give us the tools to create the lifestyle you want rather than repeating the cycle. The GOOD in the title of the book calls out that purpose: Guiding Our Own Destiny financially will give you freedom in ways you never imagined possible.

CHAPTER 1

ENVIRONMENT

While you and I might not have grown up together, I'm sure we could have a lot in common. I was born into circumstances that were less than ideal for any student. From a very young age, I was taken in and raised by my grandparents. Like many, I don't come from a perfect family situation, but I chose to make the best of my circumstances instead of letting my circumstances make the worst of me. And I need you to do the same thing. Even if your upbringing as a student has its fair share of hardships, you can choose to have different experiences as an adult. Although you could not choose the hand you were dealt early in life, you can choose how you play it. Even though your options might be temporarily limited, choose to play to win.

A common denominator for the choices available and the experiences you will have in life will be rooted in your finances: no matter your career field, gender, race, or religion, your finances will play a critical role. More times than not, when you are raised in less-than-ideal circumstances, money is not available in abundance. The lack of available cash tends to add additional stress to already unfortunate situations. Because I was exposed to so much financial struggle growing up, I started to see it as a normal part of life. However, there was always a part of me that didn't want to accept that as normal, and it is my hope that you don't want to accept financial struggle as a normal, everyday part of life either.

My environment was subconsciously teaching me that the only way I would become financially stable would be through the *D.E.A.*: dealing *drugs*, becoming an *entertainer*, or making it to the league as a professional *athlete*. I need you to understand that you can become extremely wealthy without a ball, a microphone, or pedaling poison to your community. The richest among us made their money through owning assets such real estate, stocks, and/or businesses. Ownership is a result of mental rather than physical attributes. Therefore, your level of thinking is vital when it comes to your quality of life. This is why the wealthy invest so much of their time and money into learning and the broke people I know don't spend much time or money learning much of anything significant. Let me share with you a few things about the broke people that I know.

The Broke People I Know

It's common for broke people not to read books that are not a part of work or school requirements. They own more televisions than they do books. They waste more time scrolling on social media, arguing over celebrities' personal affairs than they do working towards their own dreams. They are caught up on all their TV shows and movies but not their bills. They tend to complain about their circumstances a lot while never taking responsibility to change them. They're always the victims, it's always someone else's fault because they're broke. The earlier you hold yourself accountable for the choices you make, the sooner you'll be able to change your circumstances. Your parents, your teachers, your counselors, and your mentors can help you, but at the end of the day, it's up to you to create the kind of life you desire to live.

Self-sufficiency is the best form of dependency as you strive towards success in life. No one else is coming to save you from struggling financially: your money will always depend on you. I learned that early in life, and I need you to accept this, too.

Self-sufficiency is a trait that I learned from being raised by my grandparents. Being told "No" so much when I asked for things taught me that if I wanted something I would have to work for it. I got my first job right after I turned 15, and I've been working ever since. I never had an issue with working; my problem was that I was working towards the wrong things. As a student, my only goals for my money were to buy clothes, shoes, and have money for the canteen at school. All I knew about money at the time was to make a dollar, save a dime, and spend the rest. I can't tell you how many times I've heard, "You work hard, enjoy that money." That was the motto of the broke people that I knew.

I knew from an early age that I didn't want to struggle financially. My problem, like most people, was having and applying the right information about money. The environment I grew in taught more about fashion than finances. We were striving to be fresh from head to toe, and spending every dollar we had to do it. By the end of this book, you will have the understanding of how to make your money work for you rather than working for money and having very little to show for it. The wealthiest among us have their money work for them through assets, and *then* they spend the money their assets make them. When I was a teenager, I didn't have the slightest idea about my money making me money.

I didn't have anyone in my ear to tell me to learn about money, stack my money, or invest my money. My friends and I didn't talk about investing, at home investing wasn't a discussion with my grandparents, and even in school we didn't learn about money from instructors. It wasn't until years after struggling financially as an adult that I started to learn about money and how to make it work for me. As a student, the only way I knew how to make money was to go to work and punch the clock for as many hours as I could.

The majority of people who struggle financially wouldn't struggle if they learned about and applied the correct information with their money. This is why you must place high value on your environment and education. In this information age, you can get in the right environments through physical books, audiobooks, podcasts, and even YouTube series. When everyone around you has no hopes or specific plans to end their financial struggles, living paycheck-to-paycheck becomes a normal part of life. And that's the kind of life that I don't want for you. The knowledge you do or don't possess will make or break your experiences in life.

My GPA was much lower than what it should have been, not because I wasn't smart, but I didn't see the value in challenging myself. My teenage mind was telling me "you only need a 2.0 to play sports", so I didn't strive harder academically. My biggest downfall of applying minimum effort is that it became automatic. And when you put forth a minimum effort, you get minimum results. Minimum results will lead you to minimum options and choices in life. That leads to someone else having control of the decisions you want to make. And when someone else is making the important decisions about your life, they're going to do it with *their* best interest in mind, not yours.

The environment of growing up paycheck-to-paycheck was recreated in my own adult life. This is exactly the type of lifestyle I don't want you to even start. You won't always be a teenage student, but you will always use money. My goal is to get you to commit to becoming a student of wealth at an early age. And avoid years of financial hardship. As I travel to various schools and organizations to conduct workshops on personal finances I've never met a student with burning desires and dreams of struggling financially as an adult. Another question I ask is: "What can you tell me about money?" No matter the school or organization the responses are always the same because the environments are similar.

"Money is tight", "Money is hard to come by", and "Bills are taking all of my money." These were responses from teenagers but sounded just like full time working adults living paycheck-to-paycheck. You have already been learning about money whether you realize it or not. It's up to you to gain a better understanding of how money can benefit rather than burden you. Therefore, we have to identify if the information we learn and apply will lead us closer to or further away from our ideal financial lifestyle.

CHAPTER 2

INCOME

In his best selling book, *Rich Dad Poor Dad*, Robert Kiyosaki explained that there were 4 different ways to make money, which are by being: an employee, self-employed, a business owner, or an investor. These are the categories that make up the cashflow quadrant, but regardless of what category you are in or soon-to-be in, you're going to need a plan for your money. And that's all a budget is: it's simply a plan for your money. Don't think of a budget as a source of restriction but rather as a GPS guiding you to your financial destination. I personally found that the people who don't plan their money before they get it typically don't have much money. Budgeting is the art of directing your money before you get it instead of wondering where it went after it's all gone. Ben Franklin is quoted as saying, "By failing to plan, you are preparing to fail." You should always have a plan for your money. **No matter how much money you currently have, your next dollar should always have a destination.** Whether it's saving for new shoes, saving for your first car, or saving for college, always have a plan for your money.

Create the habit of planning your money as a student and it will be easier for you as an adult. Now, when I was a student none of my teenage peers and myself included was making any kind of budgets or plans for our money because that wasn't the normal thing to do for our environment. The normal thing was to get paid, and then go shopping, which is a habit many students take into adulthood. The only plans that we knew about money were paying bills. If you want to be successful in the area of your money, your plans must exceed rent, car notes, and lights. Create a budget that aligns with your present day and future goals. When people don't have a future for their money through planning, it's easier for them to spend it. Now let's cover some common budget options that most people use.

The most common types of budgets are zero-based budgets, percentage-based budgets, and envelope-based budgets. A *Zero-Based Budget* is when your entire income is planned out all the way down to $0.00. This means that every dollar out of your paycheck has a destination. A *Percentage-Based Budget* is when your income is divided by a certain percentage for a certain area. For example, let's say you have a $500 paycheck from your job and let's divide that into 4 areas: clothes, car, college, and cash. So, this means that 25% ($125) will go towards new clothes and/or shoes; $125 will go towards saving for your first car; $125 will go towards saving for your college fund; and $125 will be available for cash on hand.

An *Envelope-Based Budget* is when all your money is divided with cash into different envelopes. For example, you could have an envelope for eating out, and once all the cash is gone from that envelope you stop eating out. Develop a budget that's going to work for you and your goals. Any form of budgeting is going to require your discipline, so you must keep your future goals in mind. The more you budget, the easier it will become.

Think about it like this: having a budget is simply planning the money you have coming in and going out. Some critical components of any budget are cash flow, variable expenses, and fixed expenses.

Your cash flow is calculated by your total income minus your total expenses (Income-Expenses=Cash Flow). This is the area lenders will look at when it comes to making lending decisions, but they might refer to it as your debt-to-income ratio. Always strive to keep your income as high as possible while keeping your expenses low. Aim to stay at a debt-to-income of 50% or better. Meaning, if your income is $1,000 a month, don't allow your bills to go over $500 per month. This will provide you some financial breathing room for the unexpected. Variable expenses are bills that fluctuate up and down every month. An example would be a light bill because the amount due will change every month depending upon how much electricity is used. Fixed expenses are bills that stay the same every month. An example of that would be a car payment. Now, let's dive a little deeper into the breakdown of a common paycheck.

When I received my first paycheck, I realized that somebody had already got some of my money before I did. The amount of income you have before taxes is known as *Gross Income*. The money you actually take home after taxes is known as *Net Income*. I had to ask myself, "Who's F.I.C.A.?" F.I.C.A. stands for Federal Insurance Contributions Act. It's a federal payroll tax that's deducted from each paycheck. You can call this Uncle Sam, the Tax Man, or F.I.C.A., but taxes will be one of your biggest expenses as an employee. Taxes will come in many different sizes and forms and depend on where you live and what you do to generate income.

Taxes are fees charged by the government on a product, income, or activity. Some examples of taxes are income taxes, property taxes, vehicle taxes, and sales taxes. Income tax is a fee based upon the amount and type of income you make. Property tax is a fee charged based on the type and amount of land owned. Vehicle tax is a fee based on the year, make, and model of the vehicle you own. Sales tax is a fee based on the products or services we purchase. Funds generated from taxes help pay for public roads, schools, Social Security, Medicare, and public libraries, just to name a few.

As an adult, outside of your taxes you will have other typical recurring expenses, but I want to go over the top two expenses. The first expense as humans that we will always need is some place to stay. Paying a mortgage or rent is commonly the biggest expense for most people coming out of their net income. When I was a student, I had a deep desire to move out and get my own place to live. But, I advise you that if you're living in a safe and stable environment, stay there and stack your money. The money that you would be paying in housing could be used to lead you to an early retirement instead.

The second biggest expense I've seen of net income would be transportation. Depending on where you live, you may always need to have your own car, but I've seen too many adults get cars that they truly can't afford. I've worked with adults whose transportation cost was just as much as their housing cost. When it comes to cars, you have to factor in insurance, maintenance, fuel, taxes, and the car note itself if the car is financed. If you can keep these two expenses as low as possible for as long as possible, you can have more cash flow to invest, have new experiences, or avoid the stress of having to cover those bills.

CHAPTER 3

DEBT

Debt is one of the biggest obstacles when it comes to building your net worth. The moment you spend borrowed money that you haven't earned, you go into debt. Avoid, as much as possible, the purchasing of products or services on borrowed money. Financing is the provision of funding. So, when you decide to finance products or services, you're getting someone else to pay upfront, and you commit to paying the money back. I used to look at not having to pay in full upfront as a good thing, but I wasn't considering the total amount I would end up paying back. Typically when lenders are loaning out money, they're not doing it out of the kindness of their hearts. Lenders are businesses or people that loan money to make a profit. Your decision to borrow will produce profits for the lender(s). Let's go through an example: instead of paying $500 for a product or service upfront, you could potentially make 5 payments of $100 over time.

Doesn't sound like a bad deal, right? But financing typically doesn't work like this. Most lenders will add interest and fees into the financing of product(s) and/ or service(s). More realistically, you'll be paying more than 5 payments of $100, it could look more like 5 payments of $112, which would put you at a total of $560 for a $500 product or service. In this example, you see that financing is a way that companies generate additional profits just from giving customers the option to make payments.

I can't tell you how many times I've seen both the lenders and the customers focus solely on the minimum payment due. As a lender, the longer it takes to pay off, the more money I make. But as a customer, the longer it takes to pay off, the more money it costs me through interest and fees. Debt is a big hindrance when it comes to your ability to be able to build wealth. So many people have so many payments due that they don't have the option of keeping any of their income to themselves. They are making payments to all of their accounts except the ones that actually build their wealth. Never become a big spender on borrowed money.

Balling on borrowed money is a path that will lead you to being broke and struggling financially. I've also learned that some people are okay with struggling financially as long as it looks like they're balling. Some don't mind borrowing and blowing money just to give the appearance of having big money. **Looking like big money is a broke man's sport and I've met some professionals.** Prevent going into debt by not financing things you really don't need and really can't afford. Jay-Z said "if you can't buy it twice, you can't afford it."

While you're in the process of growing your wealth, your level of discipline is going to have to be greater than your desire(s) for pleasure. Even if you have the money or have the ability to borrow the money, you don't because you have a bigger goal in mind than having fun. There's a group of people that doesn't have discipline when it comes to finances and this is why they continue to go deeper into debt. Lack of discipline plus a great desire for pleasure is a recipe lenders love. Instant gratification and no money equal more profits for lenders. In most cases when you go to borrow, you are agreeing to pay more money for a product or service over time because you don't have the money to pay up front. Lenders make money off selling the original product or service, and they make additional money adding interest and fees to the product or service. These are two different ways that lender's are generating income off of the same one item. The more you can avoid financing products or services, the better off your finances will be.

The original amount that's being borrowed is known as the principle amount. The interest is the amount of money that lenders charge you in order to borrow that principal amount. A fee is an additional payment that lenders charge and doesn't reduce the principal amount. Some examples of fees are: an origination fee–a fee that's charged to start your loan; an annual fee–a fee charged by some lenders on an annual basis; A late fee–a fee charged when the payment is made after the due date; and an overdraft or over the limit fee–a fee that's charged when you have spent more money than you had available. Fees and interest rates will vary based on what product or service is being financed and the lender who's doing the financing.

Two of the biggest factors in determining your interest rate will be the principal amount borrowed and your credit rating. The higher your credit score(s), the lower your interest rate. This is because you are less of a risk in the eyes of the lender. And you are more attractive to other lenders as a borrower, so they will offer competitive rates to win your business.

In the event that you must borrow, be very selective and cautious before signing any agreement to take on new debt. Identify the total cost of borrowing, not just the minimum payment due. Calculate the principal, interest rate, and any fees for your total figure before you decide to finance. Put as much of your own money into the product or service as you can from your savings in order to borrow the least.

Your aim should be to have all 3-credit scores as high as possible and the amount borrowed as low as possible. We will cover credit more in detail later in this book. But, for now, keep these goals in mind. I personally believe if more people identified the total cost before financing they would be less likely to borrow. Your goal should be to generate interest on your money, not pay it out. Albert Einstein is quoted as saying, "Compound interest is the 8th wonder of the world. He who understands it earns it... he who doesn't... pays it."

If you're not careful, the interest on the loan(s) you take out could far surpass the original amount you borrowed. This is a common problem with some student loan borrowers. Even on some financial products the interest rate will change, this is known as a variable interest rate. This is a common trait with credit cards. This means that you can make a purchase using your credit card at one interest rate, and the interest rate could increase before you even finish paying it off. The price increasing after you make the purchase isn't the best way to shop in my opinion. Making late payments could also result in an interest rate increase.

This is known as a penalty interest rate. To reduce the amount of interest that you would pay for borrowing, focus on getting the highest amount possible to the actual principal, not just making the payment. Most payments are composed of principal and interest. The money that's paid in interest doesn't reduce the principal amount, that's the lender's profits. Identify exactly how much of your payment would be going to the principal and increase that amount as much as your finances will allow.

Making your payment before the due date will be another good habit in order to practice to prevent paying additional money in late fees. Identify what's known as your statement date and aim to make your payment by that date. The statement date is when your lender will report your payment history and balance to the credit bureaus. Aim to make your payment before your due date and pay more than the minimum amount due: these are two goals to always strive for when making payments. You should avoid getting into debt as much as you can, but if you must borrow, be strategic and have a plan for repayment. Don't just borrow simply because you can. Remember, the more you borrow and the longer you take for repayment will result in you paying more profits to the lender(s), which, in turn, will result in having less money for your own financial goals and dreams.

Getting into debt by spending borrowed money is not a decision to be taken lightly. You truly reduce your financial options when you spend money that you haven't yet earned and have to pay back with interest. Avoid the habit of spending potential money: this is the money that you could potentially make if your plans go your way. My Grandpa used to tell me, "Don't count your chicks before they hatch." And I'm telling you to steer clear of spending your money before you make it. Some of the most common forms of debt for students are: student loans, credit cards, vehicle loans, and high interest personal loans. Most of which, if not all, could be avoided through strategic planning in advance. Let's discuss each of these areas in further detail.

STUDENT LOANS ARE NOT FREE MONEY! Student loans are a very profitable business model, key word being business. These are loans that are made for the purpose of financing higher education. But if you're not careful, this can be one of the most expensive decisions you could ever make. At the time of this writing, according to Forbes, student loan debt is at 1.75 trillion dollars. When it comes to paying for college, student loans should be your last option. And of this option, borrowing the lowest amount possible is absolutely critical. Every $1 you don't have to borrow is a win. If your family finances are anything like mine were, there's a strong chance that you will have to borrow, but the priority here is to borrow the lowest amount possible and pay the loans back as soon as you possibly can.

The 3 most common ways to pay for college expenses are your own money, free money, and borrowed money. Now of these 3 options, which option sounds best to pay for your college expenses? If you're thinking of free money, then you and I are on the same page! Free money for college expenses comes in the forms of grants and scholarships. Identify and locate a team of people who will prioritize locating as much free money as possible for your college expenses. There have been many students who have received well into the 6-7 figures in scholarship monies. Every dollar that you don't have to borrow is a point, and the objective is to get enough points to be able to attend college for free. And the best way to acquire more points is to build an amazing team. Recruit the best talent you can– find and build your starting 5.

Building your Starting Five

The first of your starting five would be yourself. You need to make the scholarship journey a very high priority in your life as a student. Research and reach out to previous winners for words of wisdom on how they were able to win their scholarships. And even if you don't personally know any scholarship winners, there's always the World Wide Web. Pinpoint multiple scholarships and plan your activities accordingly. What are their GPA requirements, if any, what type of community or after-school programs would they look for winners to have participation in? Make sure you can fulfill all of their requirements to meet their qualifications for winning the scholarship.

The next up of your starting five would be to ask your parents/ guardians for help. Even if they don't know anything about this process, at the very least they could hold you accountable and be a source of encouragement for you on this journey. Next up you have your high school counselors. I know you aren't the only one in your graduating class and they will have many students to serve, but I need you to stay in constant contact with your counselor(s) about pairing your goals with potential opportunities. Use their wisdom to your advantage as you're on this scholarship journey. Oftentimes when you show people you're committed to something, they respond by committing to your commitment. Next up you have your potential future financial aid coordinator. Their full-time job is rooted in knowing the details of scholarships, grants and loan packages. Let them assist you in locating all the free money for which you could possibly be qualified.

The fifth position would be that of the Trio program. If you haven't already enrolled in your local Trio program, please do your future a favor and do so. Trio will forever have a special place in my heart. I love conducting financial literacy workshops for their students and have done so across multiple Trio programs. My wife is a Trio alumna and wouldn't be where she is today if it wasn't for the guidance of the Trio program. Trio is an organization that provides assistance for low income and first generation college students for their college journey. There's my suggested starting 5 for your "Money For College Team." Feel free to add any additional members to your team as necessary. Remember the overall goal is to attend college for free or as close to free as possible.

Research any championship team or any successful business owner(s), and you'll see they all have a great team. Apply this same principle on your scholarship journey. Don't go through this process alone, especially if you come from an environment where college degrees aren't available in abundance. All of these team member's are available at no direct cost to you. Don't fall for the scams that prey on families by charging big bucks for scholarship information. Allow these free services to assist you in finding free money.

Your Money

I once went to church with a young lady who started working her first job as a teenager. The only thing was that her mom used to take most, if not all, of her paychecks every time she got paid. This process went on for years and this young lady eventually grew frustrated with always having her money taken. Could you picture yourself working on a consistent basis just to have most, if not all, of your money taken? As she finished high school and was transitioning into college, her mom had a surprise for her. It was the information to the bank account where her mom had been saving all of her paychecks from the past several years.

This young lady told us she never looked at money the same from that point on. While free money is the primary goal, saving money for your college expenses should be a part of the plan. We are going to cover savings in detail later in this book, but for now here are some things that I want you to be aware of. There's something called a 529 Plan that's offered by some employers that your parents/guardians might have access to. This plan allows for pre-tax dollars to be invested and grown tax free for the purpose of college expenses. There's also another option of something called an UTMA or UGMA Custodian Account.

These are custodian investment accounts that are established by the parents for the benefits of their children. We will also cover these accounts in detail later in this book. If these options aren't available, however, look into opening at least an online savings account. One of the benefits of the online savings is that it's not readily available like some other savings accounts. In order to access the funds, they would have to be transferred from your online account, which sometimes takes up to 24 hours. This will help prevent you from making impulse purchases that reduce your funds that are being saved for college. If the financing of your college education primarily depends on you, make and save every dollar that you possibly can.

I saved the most expensive option for last! Once again, **STUDENT LOANS ARE NOT FREE MONEY!** Before you can take out a loan with most reputable businesses, you must prove your ability for repayment. As a young adult, I've been denied small personal loans, credit cards, and multiple vehicle loans, yet somehow I was able to get approved for tens of thousands of dollars for higher education. Lenders typically don't approve loans that they assess to be too risky, but student loans are not risky for lenders at all. So, I was able to borrow funds without having any idea as to what I was agreeing to. I want you to answer this: how much money would you lend out if the repayment were guaranteed? And the longer it took for repayment, the more profit from interest you make? How much time would you give for the repayment of the loan? It's not uncommon for the interest to far surpass the principal amount borrowed on student loans.

For the most part, repayment of student loans is pretty much guaranteed. This is why people with student loan debt typically do not have a hard time getting their loan payments paused through deferment or forbearance. Growing up, no one in my household held a college degree, so I wasn't educated on the student loan business. But I highly encourage you to learn about student loans in detail before you agree to the loan terms that you don't fully understand. There's no statute of limitations on student loan debt.

This means that student loan collections activity will continue until you have a $0.00 balance. If you still have an unpaid balance, student loan debt could cause your Social Security income to be garnished. Student loan debt could cause your regular job paychecks to be garnished. Student loan debt could cause your tax refund to be garnished. If you become disabled, your disability income can be garnished. Unpaid student loan debt could also cause you to lose your job and keep you from gaining certain employment. Outside of death and certain forgiveness programs, collection activities will always continue on unpaid student loan debt.

There are 2 types of student loans: Federal loans, also known as direct loans, which are loans that come directly from the government and must be repaid with interest and private loans, which are loans that come from credit unions, banks, schools, or other state agencies. Let's discuss private loans first and then we'll come back to federal loans. Private loans don't offer the same type of repayment options that federal direct loans offer. I remember trying to explain to my wife about having to make student loan payments while I was still a full time student, and she found that hard to believe. But this is something that is common practice with private loans.

They oftentimes require repayment of your student loan debt while you are still in school. Private student loans often require an established credit history for approval. Private student loans can't be consolidated like federal loans, but instead they must be refinanced. Forgiveness programs aren't available with private loans like they are with federal loans. Some private student loan lenders also use variable interest rates, and to have something increase in price after the purchase just doesn't sit well with me. Let's cover some information on federal loans.

There are 4 different types of federal direct loans that are made available. One type is Direct Subsidized, which is a need-based loan available for undergraduate students. The Department of Education will cover the interest on these loans while you are a student. The next type is the Direct Unsubsidized loan, which is a loan available to undergraduate and graduate students. You are responsible for the interest on these loans at all periods. The third type of loan is the Direct Plus loan, which is a credit- based loan that is available for professional students or the parents of a dependent undergraduate student. And lastly there's the Direct Consolidation Loan, which is a loan that combines all of your loans into one loan.

Cut It Close

"You keep the debt, give me the degree." These were words that a student said to me after I finished a financial literacy workshop at her school. In the event that you have to borrow to complete your higher education, take out the absolute lowest amount possible. Cut it as close to $0.00 as you possibly can! Don't do like many others and myself, get a refund check and waste it. So many students who come from circumstances similar to mine who aren't used to having access to thousands of dollars at one time get access to that cash, waste it, and have a fun time while doing it. Identify any potential work-study opportunities that might be available to you as a student.

Consider working a part-time job to cover regular living expenses and avoid taking on credit card debt. Do you have the opportunity to take college credit classes as a high school student? Can you get to your desired degree through a Bridge Program? Would you be willing to start your higher education at a local community college and then transfer to the University of your choice in order to reduce your college expenses? Can you get your same education and degree by staying in-state? Would you or your parent(s) be willing to work at your college of choice in exchange for a reduced tuition? When it comes to student loans, less is more.

Credit Cards Part 1

I received my first credit card as a full time student in the amount of $600. The amount of information I possessed on credit cards was very minimal. The only thing I knew about credit cards was that they were bad and I shouldn't use them unless there was an emergency. In fact, the only reason I started using it was because my roommate told me that if I didn't I wouldn't be able to build my credit score. After that I started to swipe and rack up credit card debt. My first purchase was a $200 TV, and after that I really can't remember much of anything that I purchased. But I know it didn't take long for me to max that credit card completely out. It's so easy to go into credit card debt when you don't fully understand what you're doing. You should never view your credit card balance as a savings balance or extra money. But instead I want you to look at your credit card as a tool to build your credit scores. And, like any tool that's used improperly, things can go wrong.

There are several different types of credit cards: you have a store card, major credit card, and a charge card. A store card is a type of credit card that can only be used at a certain store and nowhere else. For example, when I purchased my wife's engagement ring I applied for a Kay's card. After the approval for this store card, I could only use this card at Kay Jewelers and nowhere else. I couldn't use it to purchase gas or to buy food, it could only be used on products/services that particular store was offering. A major credit card is a card that can be used anywhere. Major credit cards are accepted regardless of the products or services. A charge card is a credit card that must be paid in full, down to a $0.00 balance every month. Before you apply for any credit card you must be able to answer a few questions.

The first one: why do you need this card? Next, does this card report to all 3 credit bureaus? Next up, what will my potential interest rate be? After that, does this card offer any reward(s)? Rewards are benefits that some credit cards offer to get you to use your card more. Some examples of rewards include cash back, air travel miles, discounts, early purchases, reduced interest, etc. Lastly, is this a major credit card that I could use at any business?

According to CNBC, the average credit card debt is $6,194. Don't become the average person. Credit cards are super convenient to use on most purchases by not requiring you to have the money at the time of purchase. Unlike cash, credit cards allow you to shop anywhere in the world regardless of your physical location via the Internet. You also don't even have to have the full amount of your purchase(s) as long as you have the availability on your credit card. Major credit cards will only charge you a portion of the amount you charged to the card, which is called a minimum payment. The bigger your total balance due and the longer you take to pay it off the more profits for the credit card companies. The goal of the credit card provider is to produce a profit. Your goal as the cardholder will be to build your credit without going into debt. One of the biggest ways to accomplish this goal: don't allow your swiping to exceed your available cash balance. Don't charge any purchases on your credit card(s) that you don't have in cash. According to LendingTree.com, the average credit card interest rate is 19.55%. So for every $1.00 you swipe you could potentially have to pay back $1.20 all in the name of convenience.

As a student in the process of establishing your finances, every single dollar matters. Exercise discipline and allow interest to work in favor of building wealth and not against you by getting you deeper in debt. When you use your credit card(s), you will receive your credit card bill within 30 days with a due date. The due date is the absolute last day that you have to make your payment before additional fees accrue. Your credit card company could charge you an additional late fee and/or charge you a higher penalty interest rate. Ideally, you would want to make your payment as soon as your finances allow. There's also something called the statement date. This is when the credit card companies will report your activity to the credit bureaus. Identify your statement date with your credit card company. They typically fall before your due date.

For example, your payment due date is the 20th, but your statement date could be the 11th. You want your reported balance to the credit bureaus to be as low as possible. Consider only charging money that you were going to already spend anyway. This will give you the credit history without adding any additional debt. Here's what that looks like: you have $40 cash to spend on new clothes. You charge that $40 on your credit card first, and then you use the $40 to pay off the credit card balance. This will give you the history without adding on any new debt.

New Car Struggle

One of the biggest pleasures you can experience is that of having your own car. I'm from South Carolina where there is no massive public transportation system like you would find up north. When I was a student, having your own car equaled freedom and popularity. It didn't even matter what condition the car was in! As long as you were rolling, you were relevant. Increasing my social status as a student wasn't my main goal, though. I really just wanted to get back and forth without having to ask for rides every time. Whether it was going to games, movies, work, or going to hang out with friends, pulling up driving just felt so much better as the driver rather than a passenger being dropped off. After practice during high school my grandpa used to have me waiting for hours before He came! That was not fun!

The only thing worse than being a high school student with no car is being a high school graduate with no car. If you don't like asking for rides as a teenager, then you're going to hate it as a young adult. When you're in high school, having a car is a luxury, but as you get older, having a car is a necessity. In South Carolina, a dependable car equaled a dependable income. Without having a dependable income could place you in desperate situations, and people in desperate situations often make desperate financial decisions. Whether it's the high payments on a new car or consistent maintenance issues on a lemon. Students who don't come from wealth and don't have clear plans on their finances often choose vehicles that cost them too much. I personally as a young adult had tunnel vision for a new car with rims and all the luxury trimmings. But, as you are establishing your finances, owning expensive cars shouldn't be your mission. Two of the main questions you need answered before you purchase are: "Can I really afford this vehicle" and "Is this reliable?" Have this conversation with yourself, mentor(s), and trusted family members who are good with money.

I can't tell you how many times I've seen car payments block people from buying their first house, having peace of mind, and improving finances overall. Transportation costs could be one of your biggest stumbling blocks to establishing your wealth if you allow it. The goal at this point in your life is to get from Point A to Point B safely, not in style. I'm telling you this from years of experience: please don't make the same mistakes I made. As a young full-time firefighter, I was paying almost half of my monthly income just on transportation. I had a new truck note, a new motorcycle note, maintenance costs, fuel, and insurance that I had to cover every month. This was money I could have used to build my investment account(s) and that could still be generating an income for me all these years later. I was riding around in style while struggling financially. **Riding clean should be the by-product of the wealth you built, not the priority of the majority of money you make.**

When you are looking into getting a new car, you must calculate all the vehicle costs to truly identify if you can afford the car. There's the actual cost of the car itself: what's the asking price for this vehicle? If you're financing a new car, what's the interest rate? Take your monthly payments and multiply it by the life of the loan to get a better view of how much you'll be paying for the car over the complete term. Research similar makes and models to qualify whether or not you're getting a good deal. Use research tools such as Kelly Blue Book, Carfax, Google, and Carmax just to name a few. Do you live in a State in which you have to pay property taxes? If so, how much? Call and receive multiple quotes from different car insurance providers to verify how much your insurance will cost per month. It will be to your benefit to keep your driving record as clean as possible. Accidents, speeding tickets, DUI violations, reckless driving violations, and being under 25 will all play major factors in determining your rate.

Be mindful not to overlook maintenance costs as well. Calculate how much new tires, brake jobs, and oil changes cost, to name a few. Also, is this a type of vehicle that an average mechanic can repair or is this dealer specific? How many miles are on the car right now and how many miles could it potentially get out of the life of the car? How old is this car? Ask a family mechanic to look over the car to verify what kind of shape the car is in. If you're in a position to, don't go at this process alone. Let someone who truly has your best interest at heart, and not a sales commission, assist you. You now have many different factors to consider before getting a new car, use them all.

Bad Money Bankers

The absolute worst time to borrow money is when you don't have any of your own money. And it doesn't help the situation if you have bad credit and don't have many financial institutions to borrow from. The more you can prove to a lender that you don't really need their loan, the better terms you'll be offered in order for them to win your business. Lenders typically want their loans with the best potential customers because their money isn't at as much of a risk. So lenders will compete with each other by offering better terms on financial products to win business. The number one goal for your money should be to have your money make you more money, and this is the same principal with lenders.

People who have a proven track record will typically get offered even more money. Someone who manages their credit card(s) well will get offers from other credit card companies. Someone who manages their vehicle loan well will often get more offers on new vehicle loans. Think of which person you are likely to loan your own money to: the person who has a history of always paying their loan back or the one who has a history of not paying it back but needs it more? I grew up around a lot of good, kind-hearted people, but they had less than ideal financial circumstances. And lenders make decisions based on financial credit history not good hearts. There are established businesses whose sole mission is to serve customers with less than ideal financial circumstances. And because these people don't have many financial intuitions they can turn to for loans, they charge them extremely high rates.

I've personally witnessed loved ones pawn their prized possessions for far less than what the items were worth only because they really needed the money. I've seen people who I care deeply about struggle between bad and worst choices when it came to these bad money bankers. To this day, I don't do business with pawnshops, payday advances, title loan companies, or appliance rent to own places. Some of these businesses aren't even legal in all 50 states! I've never personally seen any of these businesses actually improve my loved ones' circumstances: they only made them worse.

More than likely there will come a time in your life when you'll have to borrow money, and I understand that. I just want you in a position so that you'll never have to do business with any of these places that take advantage of your situation. When you are running low on finances, I want you to consider ways to increase your income, not getting a loan. Only borrow money when absolutely necessary, not as a means to experience some forms of pleasure. As I watched my loved ones make these bad money transactions, it was never for a lot of money. It was typically around a few hundred bucks, which, I understand, is a lot for some people. Build your savings for unexpected financial hardships to keep you out of going deeper into debt by using these places.

With *Payday Advance Loans*, you will give these lenders permission to debit your account for the amount you need to borrow plus their fees. In the event that you can't make your payment by the original due date; you could request the option to extend the payment for an additional fee. So, at that point, you would owe the original amount you borrowed, original fees, plus the new fees for extending the loan. Remember, interest is one of the most critical factors when it comes to borrowing money. You must completely understand how much you are being charged to borrow before you take out any loan(s). According to the Federal Trade Commission, the average APR on a credit card is 15%. The average APR on a Payday Loan is 391%.

Car title loans are also an extremely expensive financial decision. These companies will allow you to take out these high interest loans using your vehicle as collateral. In other words, if you fail to repay your loan, you will lose your car. Losing your transportation is even an option when you are making partial payments. Yes, you can lose your car for not being able to make your payment in-full. And if they sell your vehicle for more than you owe, they will keep the profits. It's a win-win situation for these lenders! Either you repay the loan at 20 times an average APR or you lose your vehicle.

I moved to Orlando, FL for my higher education after I finished high school on a very limited budget. I'm not sure on the exact amount, but it was somewhere around $750. So without a lot of cash to spare and living in a new city, I fully furnished my new apartment from an appliance rental company. Like most people, I was unaware of the financial decision I was making and I was only thinking about the minimum payment and not the total payout.

It would be better for you to go without that new furniture or appliances than to sign one of these rent to own agreements. Family, friends, thrift stores, or your local church could be some of the best places to locate some of these items for free. This is a multibillion-dollar industry that sells items at 2-3 times what you would pay at a regular retail store. Their biggest selling points are no credit check required and small minimum payments.

While pawn shop loans aren't as bad as Payday and Title Loan Companies, they still aren't good options. Pawn shops will, on average, lend 25%-50% of what they can resell your item to another buyer for. For example, let's say you pawn your video game system that can be resold for $400; the amount that you could borrow would be around $100-$200. Like the previously mentioned bad money bankers, pawn shops will also charge you additional fees for these loans and any extension of the loan that you might need. According to the National Pawnbrokers Association, the average loan amount borrowed from pawnshops is $150.

As a young adult who's establishing your finances, it's a high chance there will be times when you will need to borrow money. What I don't want for you to do is make a bad financial decision and make it worse by borrowing from the wrong lenders. These bad money bankers are all billion-dollar industries: they will be okay without your money! These small loans aren't worth the additional stress that they could cause you. When an unexpected expense arises and you need fast cash, please don't turn to these businesses as an option. Start to build your savings so that you won't have to borrow. Build your credit before you need it and so that if you must borrow, you can do so at a good rate.

CHAPTER 4

CREDIT

Credit is a 3-digit number that can be your biggest asset or your greatest liability, and I've been on both sides. Having it as an asset to work for you is much greater than having your scores work against you. As a kid I came to the realization that credit was some kind of sickness the way I heard most adults talking about it. Credit was always talked about in a negative light and never as a resource. Do yourself a favor and establish and maintain good credit as a student. Credit is your ability to borrow. Another way to think about it is that credit is your financial reputation. It's what lenders look at to determine how likely you are to honor your commitments financially. Lenders are not in the business of losing money and your credit profile will dictate whether you can be trusted with their money or not. Think about it like this: would you allow someone to borrow your money that has a high chance of not paying you back?

The best time to start building your credit is before you actually need it. Your goal isn't just to get your loan approved: your goal is to get approved at the best rates and terms available. Having good credit is critical in order to get the best deals the market has to offer. Businesses that cater to people with bad credit are a multi-billion dollar industry, and they don't need any of your money. When you go to borrow, do it from a reputable, established financial institution and not some bad money banker with extremely high interest rates. Now, there are some financial guru's that will tell you to pay cash for everything and not take on debt, but, unless you are coming from a rich family, you are going to have to borrow money at some point in your life. When that time comes, it's best you borrow with good credit. And I'm going to show ways to build your credit without taking on a bunch of new debt.

5 Components Of Credit

William Fair and Earl Issac developed a business using computer software that would predict the likeliness of lenders getting repaid in the 1950's. This is where the FICO Score originates, and your FICO score can range from 300-850. The lower your score the less likely you are to repay the lender. And the higher the score the more likely you are to repay the lender and you'll have access to the best terms and rates available. The 1st of 5 components that makes up your credit score is your *Payment History*. This accounts for 35% of your credit score and is the biggest component of the 5.

This is why if you miss one or are late with one payment your score drops so significantly. If you're ever in a position where you are choosing which bill you're going to pay, pay the one that's being reported on your credit. The 2nd of the 5 components that makes up your credit score is *Amounts Owed*, which comes in at 30% of your score. This shows the lenders how much was borrowed/charged compared to how much is still owed. The lower amount you owe, the better for your credit rating.

The 3rd of the 5 components is *Credit Length* and this makes up 15% of your score. This is where you have a proven track record over a long period of time. Think about the top athletes and entertainers. Chances are they've been performing at a high level for years. The longer you can keep your financial obligations without dropping the ball, the better your credit score will be. The 4th of the 5 components that make up your credit score is *Credit Mix* and it's 10% of your credit score. This is where the lenders want to see you honor multiple or a mixture of accounts on time without overextending yourself. An example could be you having a personal loan, car note, and a credit card without missing or being late on 1 payment to any of them. The last component of your credit score is New Credit and it makes up 10% of your score. Think about someone who is always asking you or someone else to borrow money. Are you likely to lend this person money? Probably not! This is the same way a lender would look at it as well. When someone is always applying for new credit, this is a red flag for lenders. Other terms for applying for new credit are also known as a hard pull, financing, and/or a credit inquiry.

Credit Report

As a student you have your transcript that shows all of your classes, grades, and provides your GPA for all of your classes. Your transcript shows schools how well you managed your education. This is the same way to think about your credit report(s). But, in this case your credit report(s) are showing lenders how well you manage your monies. Once a lender pulls your credit reports, the reports will be all the information the lender needs to make a lending decision. Information such as your full name, Social Security Number (SSN), Date of Birth (DOB), credit accounts, credit limits and current status, and collection accounts. Always do your best to never let an account go to collections. This is one of the easiest ways to destroy your credit scores after years of building up your credit. Lenders will collect and send your credit information to the *Major Reporting Bureaus: Equifax, Experian, & Transunion*. These are the *Big 3* that will report your established credit history, good or bad.

Only trust the information about your credit report that you get directly from 1 of the *Big 3*. Other credit reporting data isn't as accurate as getting it directly from these sources. I've personally seen accounts being reported inaccurately, accounts not reported at all, and scores that were 70-100 points off from secondary sources. The majority of lenders use FICO Scores when making lending decisions. And as you're establishing your credit, you need to use accurate FICO reporting sources. If you're going to be making regular, recurring payments on something, use it to build your credit scores. Before you borrow any money, ask the lender if they report to all 3 bureaus and if they report every 30 days. All lenders don't report every 30 days and to all 3 bureaus because it costs them money to report the data, so select the lenders that will report to all 3 bureaus every 30 days.

As a consumer you also have the right to dispute any fraudulent or inaccurate information on your credit report. According to the Federal Trade Commission, 1 out of 5 people have an error on at least one of their credit reports. You can get a free copy annually of your credit report from annualcreditreport.com, or you can also enroll in a credit-monitoring program to help reduce the chances of inaccurate information getting on your credit report. Consider using monitoring from the brand names you know such as experian.com or equifax.com.

The Fair and Accurate Credit Transactions Act was designed to protect the public. This is the law that prevents inaccurate, incomplete, or fraudulent accounts from being reported. Stated another way: everything on your credit report has to be 100% verifiably yours, and if it's not it must be deleted. It is your right to dispute any and all inaccurate information that's on your credit reports. The dispute process is when you are asking the credit bureaus to investigate and verify whether or not certain accounts or information that's on your credit report is actually yours. It's best to start your dispute process by certified mail and not emails. This way you'll have physical copies and records of everything. Once your investigation starts the credit bureaus will have 30-45 days to respond to your investigation request. Don't use a copy and paste template that can easily be found online.

These letters could be marked as frivolous and not taken seriously, and I know this to be true because this is what actually happened to me. The very first time I sent a dispute letter, I received a response saying they received a "suspicious letter" and no investigation was done. If you ever have to write a dispute letter, make sure to include a copy of your ID and a bill to verify the letter is actually coming from you. Send separate dispute letters to the bureau that has the inaccurate information. So each inaccuracy receives its individual letter.

I need you to treat your credit like your life and the lives of the ones you love are depending on it because they are. Your ability to borrow, your potential employment opportunities, becoming a homeowner, getting a new car, or even your own apartment will always depend on your credit. Good credit will take years to establish but could be severely affected by 1 late payment or 1 collection account. Collection Accounts typically come after 90 days of non-payment. Companies can sell an individual debt to another party known as the collection agency. These companies are now the ones that will start contacting you for payments.

Now some collection agencies will give you some grace time for a payment and may even set up a payment arrangement before reporting you to the credit bureaus. Do your best to ensure that your accounts don't make it beyond a late payment status and into collections. Late payments are another way to significantly drop your score quickly. Past due payments are payments that are made after the due date but before 30 days. Late payments are payments that are made after the due date, grace period, and after 30 days. Past due payments will cost you more money in additional fees but late payments will cost you your credit rating.

Getting a collection account or a late payment doesn't guarantee you'll have bad credit for the rest of your life. Negative reporting credit items are just easier to prevent than it is to repair. Again, put your best foot forward to keep all negative items off of your credit. Some lenders will sometimes allow you to *skip* a payment. This is when you can put your current payment at the back of the loan. You won't be reported for being late but you will extend the life of the loan by 1 month. If you ever are reported late, sometimes you can request that your lender delete the late payment off of your credit. Some lenders will grant you this request based on your overall standing. There's something known as the pay-for-delete that you can use for collection accounts. This is when the collection account holder has agreed to have the negative account deleted off of your credit report(s) for your payment. It's best to get this agreement in writing before you make the payment. Keep this in mind: bad credit isn't ideal, but it is also not permanent. Credit reports update every 30 days, and the reason most people keep bad credit is because they accept bad credit and do nothing to improve their scores.

Credit Repair Companies

The goal is to never have bad credit, but, if you do, you have the option to repair it yourself or you can hire a credit repair company. Everything they will do for you, you can do it yourself. But, I understand the convenience of hiring someone else to do it. I've hired credit repair companies in the past and experienced both good and bad results. Be mindful that all credit repair companies aren't built the same. Some credit repair companies have their clients score improvement results as priority and other companies have their profits as their priority. Before you hire any credit repair company you want to make sure they are a legal registered company.

You only want to spend your money with reputable and honest companies. There are a lot of scammers in the credit repair industry. Some of these people will promise to get every negative item off of your credit for some huge fee. I recommend that you select a credit repair company that charges you only for the results they get for you. This means that they will only charge you for every item they can get deleted from your credit report. Also, keep in mind that there's a difference between deleted and removed.

Credit Bureaus will sometimes remove accounts as they are investigating the account. Your score can jump because the account in question isn't a factor at the moment, but once that account is verified it will end right back on your credit. When an account is removed it gives you a quick but possibly temporary fix. When an account is deleted, it's gone for good. "Deleted" is what you want your accounts in question to read on your credit report. Some credit repair companies will charge you on a monthly basis whether they are getting you results or not. You should hire a company that practices legal and ethical credit repair techniques and charges you based solely on their performance. Meaning they only charge based on what they delete, or they offer a money back guarantee if they don't improve your credit.

Build Before You Borrow

The best time to build your credit is before you need it and my favorite money to borrow is money that I don't need. Let's dig our well *before* we are thirsty. Credit cards and loans were two items I used to build my credit, but if you're fortunate enough you could use these two items plus become an *authorized user* on someone else's account. An authorized user is when you are added to an account with the authority to use the account.

The account type, payment history, account age, and balance information are all added to your credit report. This is a great method to benefit from the discipline that your family has practiced. Be mindful that you also will get the bad. Any high utilization, late, or missed payments will also be added to your credit report as well. I didn't have this option when I was your age, but it's definitely a great tool to use. As a working adult, my credit scores were once in the 400s, and I couldn't qualify for free samples. Two of the items I used to establish my good credit were loans and credit cards. Being that I was building from scratch, I had to use my own money. *Secured Loans* and *Secured Credit Cards* would help me boost my scores over 100 points within 1 year of using them.

An *Unsecured Loan* is when you can just sign your name and get approved for your desired amount, but when you haven't established your credit this is unlikely to happen with a reputable lender. An *Unsecured Credit Card* is a card that you can just sign for and get the approval, but, again, this most likely will require established credit. Since you are in or about to be in the process of establishing your credit, you will need to use your own money to secure these items. This is yet another benefit of having savings to pull from! I started with a $300 secured credit card and a $300 secured loan from two separate credit unions that reported every 30 days. How does this work? You give the lender $300 of your own money as security and are then issued the loan or credit card in the amount of $300. What I always suggest people should do with their secured loans is to place that money into their savings account and set their payments up on automatic draft. An example, if your payment is $30 a month due on the 17th, set the payment for $35 to come out on the 10th. The earlier payment date ensures the payment won't be late for holidays and weekends.

Credit Cards Part 2

Are credit cards good or bad for you? Growing up in an environment of financial hardship, I wasn't properly educated on credit cards. I was raised to believe that credit cards were only to be used in case of an emergency and to stay away from otherwise. Credit cards are a reflection of the cardholder and can be good or bad, but I stand on the side that credit cards are good for you. Major credit cards can impact all 5 components of your credit scores (Payment History, Amounts Due,

Length of Credit, Credit Mix, and New Credit). One of the critical things to be mindful of with your credit cards is your utilization rate. This shows the lenders how much of your card you actually use. And the lower your utilization rates the better.

You should always strive to never exceed 30% of your cards total balance. For example, if you have a card with a $1,000 limit, don't allow your total balance to exceed $300. When you have high utilization rates, this shows the lenders that you like to spend everything you have. And this also drops your credit scores as well. Payment history is another critical aspect of your credit scores as we discussed in *Credit Cards Part 1.* And another reminder: don't charge what you don't have the available cash to pay off. Be strategic and use your credit card(s) to build your credit scores rather than to finance shopping sprees.

Good Credit Score Recap

When a lender asks the Big 3 (Equifax, Experian, Transunion) about you, you want them to have only good things to say about your reputation. Do this by establishing multiple, positive credit reporting accounts that report to all 3 bureaus every 30 days. Keep your credit inquiries low, only have your credit pulled for financing when you plan to, never on impulse. If you have family members that you trust and they have good credit, you can be added to their credit card(s) as an *Authorized User* and benefit from their good credit. But, it's perfectly fine if you are the first of your family to establish good credit. This just means that you have to be more strategic with your money. If you don't have family members that you can lean on for good credit, turn to your personal savings.

Use your personal savings to get your first credit card(s) and loans. With your loans, redeposit that loan money back into your account. Set the payments to come out on automatic draft *before* the due date and over the minimum amount due. Start out with secured loans and then move to unsecured loans after you have established some credit and apply the same technique. You're using these loans for the sole purpose of building up and establishing your credit scores so that when the time comes that you actually need a loan, you can borrow at competitive rates.

With your credit cards, only charge what you have the available cash to pay off and with money that you were already going to spend anyway. Make your credit card payments before the due date and pay in full to avoid paying interest and/or being late. Never pay any bill late that's being reported to any credit bureau, and any bill that has to do with a lender is being reported to the credit bureaus. If it's a bill that's not being reported, use your credit card to make the payments and benefit from it's on time payments that way. Your credit rating will always make a greater ally than an enemy.

CHAPTER 5

SAVINGS

The number one complaint I receive from adults as a financial literacy educator is regrets about not having much in their savings, and this is by a landslide. Their biggest regret is that they didn't save more money in their youth. One of the biggest advantages you have right now as a student is that you have low expenses. You're more than likely not paying a mortgage, daycare, healthcare, car note, insurance, or property taxes. Use this to your advantage, and build a massive sized savings account. I once had a student tell me, "I'm young with no priorities, and I'm going to enjoy all my money now." This thought process will ensure that your savings will never grow. Most broke people I know will prioritize having fun and pleasure, and this is why they're broke. Most people I know who struggle financially come from environments where people struggle financially. It's very common for them to have absolutely no money in their possession. Most of them would consider this as a normal day, but you shouldn't. In our capitalist culture, everything is based on money. And when your money is low-to-none, so are your options. I can tell you from personal experience that not having enough money to provide for yourself and your loved ones isn't something that you will enjoy.

There's a group of people who have found comfort with having between $0.00 and not enough in their savings. Your savings will always stay around the lowest dollar amount you're comfortable with. This plays a major part in why people don't consistently grow their savings. Saving money is similar to working out, nobody else can do it for you and it requires discipline. The amount of money you make is an important component to saving money, but another critical component of your savings is actually building the habit of saving money.

If you have a consistent income and always put off saving a portion, your savings still doesn't grow. Don't build the habit of telling yourself you'll save money from the next check. Your savings is vital when it comes to investment opportunities and staying out of debt. It's your first line of defense from unexpected expenses and your first option offensively for investment opportunities. Avoiding having to borrow money and taking advantage of potential investment opportunities will all stem from your ability to save your money. According to CNBC, most working adults don't have at least $1,000 in savings, but you can reach $1,000 in savings just by saving $19.25 each week.

I Can tell you from personal experience that not having any money in savings is something to avoid. If you don't build the habit of saving money as a student, it's going to be harder for you to do it as a working adult. From personal experience, people typically don't save more as they make more money. They typically raise their expenses as their income rises. They turn bigger paychecks into bigger bills. A lot of the broke people that I know like to give the appearance of having a lot of money by buying expensive things. A lot of the wealthy people I know place a higher value in owning income-producing assets, not their personal appearance.

The very first step in building your savings up will be to identify all of your personal reasons as to why you need your savings. When your *why* is strong enough, you will always be able to identify your *how*. The number one financial goal I hear from adults is that they want to save more money. While this is not a bad goal, this is not specific enough of a goal to reach. Goals that aren't clear enough or are too generic are goals that don't get reached. You should always strive for a very specific goal when it comes to finances overall but especially when it comes to building your savings.

The next step would be to identify how much money you need. Once again: be very specific, down to the exact dollar. When you're vague on how much savings you actually need, you're less likely to reach your desired dollar amount. And as you're identifying how much money you need, do it from a place of optimism. Too many people will allow their present day circumstances to determine their future finances, and that's not the attitude I want you to have as you're establishing your savings.

As you have your total overall saving figure calculated, your next step is to break your savings goal down into smaller steps. For example, if your goal is to save $5,000, don't focus on the $5,000. Instead I want you to focus on saving $100, 50 different times. If your goal is to save $2,500, don't focus on the $2,500. Focus on saving $50, 50 different times. It was Desmond TuTu who said: "The best way to eat an elephant is one bite at a time." And this same principle holds true with building up your savings, "one" at a time. Whether it's one decision, one paycheck, or even one dollar, making the right choices over the right amount of time is the best way to go. **When you are building your savings from $0.00, ideally you should only have to do it once. Build from scratch one time, afterwards your goal should be to maintain and grow your savings.**

After you've identified *why* you need and *how much* you need to save, your next step should be to clarify your timelines. By timelines

I mean the exact date you need to reach your goal and how often you can contribute to your savings. Let's say you work a part-time job that pays you every 2 weeks, and your goal is to save $3,500 by this time next year. Your timeline would look like this: $3500 goal divided 26 paychecks would equal you saving roughly $134.62 per check for the next 12 months. When your goals and timelines are clear, you'll be less likely to waste money on things that don't line up with your goals. When you're striving to have a savings of thousands of dollars, you should move differently. You won't be able to spend like everyone else and that will be just fine. And as your savings account grows, you're going to have to be strong enough not to touch it and only share your savings goals with people who are going to help you reach them. Remember, you are working on building something that the majority of Americans haven't accomplished. It's okay to build in silence.

Now that you have your *why*, your *how much*, and your *timelines*, now it's time to identify where you're going to store your savings. I would have to tell you to look into opening an account with a FDIC insured financial institution. FDIC stands for Federal Deposit Insurance Corporation, and it was created by Congress to insure deposits made by the institution's customers. To say it another way: this is the organization that insures your money will be safe up to a certain dollar amount. The biggest problem with keeping too much cash on hand is ease of access.

There's an ease of access not only for you to spend on impulse shopping, but there's also an ease of access for someone to steal and/or lose in the event of disaster. Events such as house fires, flooding, tropical storms, hurricanes, and/or tornadoes will destroy cash money. As a young adult, I've experienced the pain of having someone steal from me. It was money I was saving for months from my regular income and also from doing freelance part-time work . I found great pleasure in watching my stash grow! Money that I thought was hidden well enough was now gone one day when I got home from work. If I had kept my money in a legal, insured, and proven financial intuition, it wouldn't have gotten stolen.

There's also an option now to have your paycheck directly deposited onto a prepaid card. My biggest dislike with some of these prepaid cards are the fees they charge. It's basically like they are charging you to use your own money, and while you are in the process of building, every single dollar matters. I'm also not a fan of keeping your savings on some of these cash transfer payment apps. I'd be too concerned with my balance disappearing or me getting locked out of my account. I know people who have had these exact issues happen with their money. Not to mention the fees some of these apps charge as well. Do your research and identify what FDIC insured intuitions work for you. Most intuitions will consist of physical banks, credit unions, and/or online-only banks.

The main difference between a bank and a credit union is what's being done with the profits. Most credit unions are non-profit member based organizations, and so they charge less in fees and share profits with its members. A credit union was the first financial institution to approve me for a loan and gave me the best options for building up my personal credit. (More tips on how I used Credit Unions to establish and build my credit will be explained in detail later in the book.) After you select an institution, you also have the option of having multiple accounts. The accounts should be set up based on your goals.

You can have a checking account that could be used for regular spending. You can also have your savings accounts where you could be building towards your first car, college expenses, or a vacation. This account should be separate from other accounts. There's also something offered by banks and credit unions called *Certificate of Deposit* or *CD* for short. This is when you're basically giving the bank a loan. You give the bank a certain amount of money and they keep it for a certain amount of time. Some benefits for a CD are higher interest rates and it's not as readily available for spending.

One of the things I hated the most about some of these big name banks was the overdraft fee. These fees are mostly associated with checking accounts but can come out of any account that's overdrawn. My biggest issue was swiping my card and the purchase not coming out of my account immediately. So my available balance would show higher than it actually was because of the previously swiped transaction that hadn't been finalized. And it was a $35 fee per transaction regardless of the amount that I spent. This is a big source of income for a lot of banks, and they don't need your money so please keep a close eye on your accounts.

Let's cover some ways you can avoid overdraft fees. First, you can tell your institution that you don't want the transaction to go through if you don't have the available balance to cover the transaction. Next, you can link separate accounts to cover any overdraft that might occur. An example would be that you have a checking and a savings linked together. And third, select your personal zero. Don't allow your account to fall below a certain dollar amount that you personally select. An example would be you'd never allow your account to fall below $200.

One of the most common questions I get asked from students is: "How much money should I save?" And my answer is always the same: it depends on your goals. While most personal finance books and gurus would tell you at least 10%. If I could go back to being a teenager, I would save at the bare minimum 50% of my check and 80%-90% on the good checks. If your current conditions won't allow you to save this much, what's the biggest amount you could save? Remember, it's going to take discipline to consistently build up your savings. And also keep in mind that most working adults don't have at least $1,000 in savings. You'll be building something that's not regular to the average person. Choosing not to spend as a student on everything you could buy will lead to more options as an adult that most people don't have. If you don't learn to build the habit of saving as a student, it's going to be harder to build as a working adult. People who wait to start saving by telling themselves they'll save more when they make more income typically don't save at that point either. When saving money isn't a priority, they just end up with bigger bills the higher their income goes.

Here's my challenge to you: I want you to save at least $10,000 by the age of 21. Don't focus on the big number; I want you to focus on the small steps. Let's say you are 16 years old, right? This means you have 60 months until you are 21. $10,000 divided by 60 months will give you $167 per month. And $167 divided by 4 will equal out to $42 a week. If you were working consistent part-time hours, would it be possible for you to save $167 a month? If you are older or younger, just calculate the months you have until you're 21 or 25, and identify how much you would need to save to reach $10,000 by age 21 or 25. Or, if you're able to save more money, aim for a goal that's higher than $10,000. Will you accept my challenge?

CHAPTER 6

INVESTING 101

It took me years to realize that my income wasn't directly linked to how hard I physically worked, so I want you to understand this principle as a student to help influence how you handle your money at an early age. Your income isn't a direct reflection of how much manual labor you can do. I was taught at an early age to work hard for my money, and that's what I did. My focus was on putting as many hours in on the job as I could. There's a group of people who work for money, and then there's a group of people who have money to work for them. You should strive to have your money working for you. Two of the biggest limitations in working for money are that we can only be in one place at a time and there's only 24 hours in a day. But, you can have your money working for you in multiple places at the same time, and your money doesn't get tired.

The way that you have your money work for you is to own income-producing assets. Owning a business that provides a product or service, owning certain forms of real estate, or owning other financial products such as stocks, Exchange-Traded Funds (ETFs), and/or mutual funds just to name a few are examples of potential income producing assets. You can own these various investments regardless of what career path you choose. For years I was only focused on *active income*, which is when you trade your time for money, but the wealthiest among us tend to focus on creating income without trading their time for it, which is known as *passive income*.

Your time is your most precious resource, and once it's spent you can't get it back. When I didn't fully understand how valuable time is, I tended to waste a lot of it. Building wealth or achieving anything of significance will require you to be very intentional with your time. Getting their money to produce a new source of income is a top priority for those intentional about building their wealth. Educating yourself on how to turn your dollars into employees is a critical component in avoiding financial hardships. The majority of broke people I know have their money unemployed via not owning any assets, and that's why they struggle.

It's hard to enjoy your time when your finances are not in order, take my word for it! Financial education should be your first step and a continuous step throughout your lifetime. Being that I was building my finances from scratch, I had to be my first and biggest investor. And if that's the case for you, too, your savings account will be your first option when you need money for your first investment(s). Building my savings account was a good habit, but getting those savings to create new income was my main objective. People who aren't properly educated on finances are usually taken advantage of on multiple fronts. Whether it's income, loans, or investments, you need to have a complete understanding before agreeing to any financial matter.

I remember back when the first stimulus checks were rolling out with most people getting at least $1200 and much more if they had kids. I must have gotten at least 5 different people ask me: "have you ever heard of a Sou-Sou?" What seemed to have gotten major popularity were people putting their money into a modern day Ponzi Scheme. It's important to know that a real Sou-Sou and a Ponzi Scheme aren't the same thing as people were framing it to be. A real Sou-Sou is a savings method mostly used by those overseas without the same banking options as others. A group of trusted friends would get together and all contribute the same amount of money until each person received the same amount that they contributed. There aren't any extremely high returns with a real Sou-Sou. For example, 5 different friends would all contribute $100 each for 5 weeks. Every week a different individual would receive the $500 payout. At the end of 5 weeks everyone in the group would have received and paid $500. A real Sou-Sou is a savings method, not an investment strategy. There's no need to recruit anyone else into the group to receive your savings back. Now let's discuss what a Ponzi Scheme is.

Charles Ponzi was an Italian immigrant that made millions of dollars in a Peter-to-Paul Scheme back in the early 1900's. He created a business promoting the framework of buying foreign postal stamps from one country and selling them in another. For example, postal stamps that were purchased in Italy could be sold in the United States for a profit. And at that time, there was a price difference in postal stamps aka postal reply coupons. FYI: the best lies tend to have some truth mixed into the story, and this was the story that Ponzi was telling would-be investors of how their money was being invested. Ponzi also promised a 50% return on investment within 45 days. Instead of flipping postal stamps, Ponzi was paying previous investors money back with new investors' money.

In order for any Scheme like this to work, there must be new money introduced into the scheme. If new money isn't introduced into the scheme, the system fails. This is why so many people were calling me and other friends: they needed new money to get their money back. For example, the scheme requires you to put up $500 and then requires you to get 2 more friends to do the same thing, and the 2 new friends have to find 2 more friends to put up $500, and so on or so forth. It promised a $4,000 payout for only a $500 contribution. Most scams promote a huge return in a short amount of time. Don't fall for their lies.

Before you invest a single dollar into any type of investment you need to be educated on the investment vehicle. Warren Buffett doesn't invest in any business that he doesn't fully understand, and you need to apply this same principle when it comes to your money. You need to understand how this business makes their money. Is this company legal and registered with the proper state and federal authorities? If this business is registered, what are some of their previous customers saying about their products or services? How long has this company been around? Who else has put their money into this investment vehicle that you would trust with your money? There's something called ROI, which stands for *Return On Investment*, this basically tells you how much money your money made you with this investment. But there's another ROI that the wealthy focus on first, which is *Return Of Investment*.

You need to know how stable your investment amount will be and the likeliness of its return before you put your money up. Right now while you're young you might not have all the money to invest, but you should make the time to learn about different investment vehicles in detail. That way when the money comes you'll be ready and educated on how to make your move and have your money working for you.

Owning your own business, real estate, and the stock market are 3 common asset classes for investing and having your money work for you. If you desire to start your own company and offer a product or service, then you should start with a detailed business plan. This is where you outline the information about all the details of your company, such as potential income, expenses, resources needed, partnerships, and marketing strategies are a few of those details.

Research and find your nearest Small Business Development Center. This is an organization that helps entrepreneurs plan, start, manage, and/or grow their business with no upfront cost. These organizations are funded by tax dollars not by your start up company. Using this organization as a form of mentorship to help you develop a solid business plan will only help your business grow. Finding mentorship is another critical component to growing your business. The biggest gap between what we want and what we have is the information that we possess. Having the right mentors will provide us the wisdom of their years without the heartache and pain they went through to learn it. Mentorship is one of the biggest and best cheat codes to success. Make it a priority to learn from those who have already achieved your life's desires.

Home Ownership 101

Real Estate Investing comes in many forms, but the most common for many is that of owning their own home. On October 28th, 2013 I closed on my very first home with money that I saved and with credit that I had to rebuild. This is an accomplishment that I'm extremely proud of still to this day. As a student, I was exposed to a lot of family and friends who were renters. Two of the biggest downfalls of renting for so long were I didn't build any equity and my stability was at the mercy of the landlord. Stability in this case refers to how much you paid for rent and also how long you could actually live there. I've heard so many stories about families having to move because the Landlord is selling the house or even increasing the rent to the point where families could no longer afford to stay.

You don't build equity simply by paying rent. Equity is the value of your ownership. For example, if you own a house that's valued at $100,000. and you still owe $40,000 on your mortgage you have $60,000 in equity. If you were to sell this house, you would receive a payout of $60,000 minus the fees associated with the closing. When you hear the word *closing,* I want you to think of a sale being finalized. *Closing* is when the funds, documents, and ownership are transferred between the buyers and sellers through the attorney's office. Before I closed on my first house, I paid rent for over 5 years. Well over $20,000 in money that I worked for went right into the pockets of another family. Let me explain some things you'll need to know to become a homeowner.

All you need to do to purchase your first house is provide the money to complete the purchase. Now you can either pay cash OR you can borrow via a mortgage to close on your first house. If you are going to have to borrow to close on your first house, you're going to need to meet all of the qualifications of the lender to get your loan approved. The first of the most common traits for lenders will be your credit history and score(s). Credit of 640 or better was a common baseline for lenders at the time of this writing. Lenders will need to look at your credit scores & history and feel secure that you will be able to repay your mortgage. Next, they would consider your debt-to-income ratio: you have to have the available cash-flow to support the mortgage you're requesting.

I've seen where lenders would approve a mortgage for 40% of the gross income. For example, if your gross (before tax) income was $3,000, you could get approved for a mortgage of up to $1,200 a month. But, as a borrower, your focus should be on what you can truly afford and not what you get approved for. Next up we have your cash reserves. Some lenders would like to see multiple months of potential mortgage payments in your savings. Next, you need to have a budget for your *Due Diligence* period. This is the timeframe where the house gets inspected to ensure everything is well with the home. Common inspections are typically a general home inspection, HVAC inspections, and termite inspection.

Lastly, we have your money for your actual closing. This would include your attorney's fees and your down payment money. Down payment money would depend on the size of the mortgage and the type of mortgage you are using. The 2 most common types of mortgages are *Conventional* and *FHA*. A *Conventional Mortgage* is a loan that's not made or backed by the government and has a down payment as low as 3%. FHA stands for Federal Housing Administration, and it's a loan that's insured by the federal government and has a down payment as low as 3.5%. The 2 most common terms of mortgages are 15-year and 30-year terms. Mortgages are cash cows for banks! The longer you take to repay, the more money they make.

Like other debt, strive to be able to pay above your mortgage payment and put that additional money towards the principal balance. One additional mortgage payment per year will save years off of a 30-year mortgage. There's also something called *PITI*, and that stands for *principal, interest, taxes, and insurance*, which is the amount you borrowed, the fee for borrowing, the taxes due to your local jurisdiction, and insurance for your home, and depending on the mortgage product you choose, this could be your mortgage payment, too.

Real Estate Investing 101

Billionaire Andrew Carnegie was quoted for saying that "90% of millionaires got their wealth by investing in real estate", so if you have a goal of getting rich, there's a high chance real estate investing is in your future. I wish I would have listened to the advice of a mentor, but I dropped the ball and it was an expensive ball at that! He told me to buy a multi-family unit and live in 1 unit and rent out the other units. This is a strategy known as *House Hacking*, and it could have created me some early age passive income. You can finance a 4-unit or under home and that is considered to be a single-family dwelling to lenders: Duplex has 2 units; Triplex has 3 units; and a Quadplex has 4 units. For example, let's say you financed a Quadplex as your first home and your mortgage is $800. You live in one unit and rent out the other 3 units for $800. That gives you a total of $2400 every 1st of the month. Now you've used your first home as a source of passive income for an additional $1,600 a month outside of your job salary. Of course the numbers will vary depending on the area you live in and style of house you choose, but this is the main concept of *House Hacking.*

Most real estate Gurus will tell you that you make your money when you buy the real estate, not when you sell. What that means for investors is that you need to find deals under their *Market Value* (i.e., what they're worth). Let's discuss some ways that you can locate some properties under what they're worth. When a homeowner doesn't make their mortgage payment over a certain amount of time, the bank will *foreclose* on their house. This is the legal process of the lender selling the house to recover the remaining money left on the mortgage. This presents an opportunity to purchase homes for under their market value because the lender is only after the remaining balance. Let's say, someone has been making his or her mortgage payments for 10 years straight and in year number 11 the house is foreclosed. During those 10 years, the house has appreciated in value and the consistent payments have taken the mortgage balance down. This is a formula for investors being able to buy houses under what they're worth. The goal is to purchase and renovate the property while still being able to produce a profit.

Another way to find homes to purchase under their market value would be locating vacant homes with out of town owners. Some of these properties will have windows boarded up, high grass, or other signs of distress. It's common that these homes were gifted to the new owners from other family members. The new owners might not be as attached to their gifted house as the previous owner or may not be willing to make repairs. This method produces an opportunity for the investor to purchase undervalued property and convince the new owner to sell this gifted house without having to make repairs. Another way to purchase houses under market value would be local government *Tax Sales*. When the homeowner doesn't pay the property taxes their local government will sell the property at auction to the highest bidder to receive the taxes owed. In my city, the homeowner has up to 1 year to redeem their house before losing it. This means that they have up to one year to make their tax payment before losing their home. Even if they redeem their house before the year is up, your winning bid will receive interest. The longer they take to redeem, the more interest your money makes. A winning bid will either get you a new house or interest on your money. But, do ALL your research before bidding!

The last method I have for you will be to get your *Real Estate License* and become a *Realtor*. Becoming a licensed professional will grant you access to learning real estate from a different perspective and price point. Most investors will make their deals with cash or access to cash within a few business days. When I was your age, there was no way I had the capital needed for real estate investing, and this might be your story as well. But, for a few hundred dollars, you could enroll in your local real estate school and begin your journey in real estate. All of these methods can be done in addition to your career and/or your college education. I want you to learn an overview about these real estate methods as a young student. This way you can position your finances accordingly and take advantage of opportunities around you. These were investment opportunities that I didn't even know existed until my 30's. If you're interested in investing in real estate, make it a priority to learn more about it.

Common Retirement Options

One day while at work I was asked the question about my retirement. I replied by saying I have the same State retirement plan as everyone else, and my coworker said, "well, what about the other one?" Seeing the confused look on my face, he began to show me his additional retirement account that was valued at over $30,000. We had started that job around the same time, and I could have been in that same position if only I had known about it.

Lord knows how much that account could be valued at now! Before we cover some common retirement options, I need you to know the exact date that you can retire. When I'm presenting, I always ask how old do you have to be to retire? And the answers are always the same: 62, 65, 70, 72, etc. But, the correct way to think about retirement is not an age but rather a dollar amount. That's right, you can retire as soon as your money will afford you the opportunity to do so. Don't spend all your years chasing money to the point where you never get to experience living outside of paying your bills. And thanks to *Compounding Interest*, the earlier you start saving for retirement, the better!

Compounding interest is when your interest starts making interest. Let's say you made 10% on a $100 investment over a 3-year period, which would now give you a new balance of $110 after year 1. Now year 2 would start with a balance of $110 and it will produce $11 for a new total of $121. And year 3 would start its balance with $121 and produce a $12.10 return for a new total of $133.10. *Compound interest* is something that can make you a lot of passive income if you understand it. There are people who have enough money invested to where they live off of the interest that their principal balance generates. Unfortunately, I know too many people who are on the paying side of compound interest instead of the receiving side.

If you start making compound interest as a teenager, how much money can you make by 35? Compounding interest is something that's at work in your employer sponsored retirement options as well. Don't delay like I did when I first started working full-time. That mistake cost me tens of thousands of dollars! Research and study all the benefits your potential employer is providing.

When you see 401k, 403b, 457, these are the tax codes for common employer retirement plans, and depending on your job, you will be told the option that's available to you. The 401k retirement plans are most common on jobs, 403b retirement plans are for the nonprofit careers, and 457 retirement plans are for the government jobs. These plans are funded with pre-tax (gross) dollars and aren't taxed until you pull them out. Now you might be thinking, "what if I want to pay for my taxes up front instead of waiting?"

This is where you would look into setting up a ROTH style account. Whether it's a Roth 401k, Roth 403b, Roth 457, it's now common for employers to offer ROTH options within their benefits packages. You also might have the option within your retirement benefits to choose what's called a *Target Date Fund*. This is a fund that will rebalance the levels between growth and stability by a certain date. In other words, the further away the target date, growth will be the priority. As you get closer to retirement (i.e, the target date), protection of funds will be more of a priority by selecting investments that are more stable.

You also might have the option to purchase your company's stock at a discount, depending on your employer. For example, you work for *Company 123* and their stock sells at $100 per share, but as an employee you have the option to purchase that same stock at $75. Now you have just bought a $100 asset for only $75 giving you $25 in equity for every share you purchase. That's also a 25% return on your money! Now if you just so happen to work for an organization that doesn't have any of these options, there's still hope. You can start your own *Individual Retirement Account* (i.e., IRA) with a brokerage of your choosing. Do your own research to identify what brokerage would work best for your situation. You also need to do your own research when it comes to selecting different retirement and investing products because at the end of the day, nobody is going to care about your retirement like you would. I would hate for you to lose your hard earned money based on someone else's bad decisions.

Financial education will always be a critical factor in society. If we want to live at a higher quality of life, we must first think at a higher quality of life.The way to improve your thinking will be through education, and your financial education should have no finish line. The more you learn and apply what you've learned about money, the harder you can make it work for you. The more you allow your money to be unemployed, the harder you will have to work. I've seen too many good people struggle because of the lack of financial information and procrastination of the financial information they did have. Most people would agree that they need to save and invest money, but they choose to do it later. Later unfortunately will end up costing the ability to afford their dreams and goals. Do not be like most of the broke people I know. Start today as a student by learning and applying the correct financial education so you won't have to struggle like a lot of working adults.

CHAPTER 7

STOCK MARKET 101

I was a 19-year-old full-time student when my instructor told the entire class how excited he was about his latest purchase. He had just bought shares of a surefire stock that was certain to change his financial future forever. He then told us that shares were trading for a fraction of a penny. He had a massive amount of shares, and he had just needed the value of the shares to reach $1.00 each. After listening to him, I opened my first brokerage account and made my very first stock purchase by investing in this company as well, but the hopes of an early retirement soon faded as the company went out of business and took my money with it.

At this time in my life, I knew very close to nothing about the stock market. I had only heard stories about how risky and complicated stocks were. I was told I could lose all of my money. And to make matters worse, these stories that I was hearing came from people who did not and had never owned any stocks. When you grow up in an environment where everyone is just trying to survive financially, the stock market isn't a hot topic of discussion. I missed out on a lot of money because I wasn't exposed to stocks at an earlier age. Don't make the same mistake I did by avoiding learning about stocks. The very first thing I should have done before investing my money was done my own research. Before you invest your money into anything, invest your time by researching qualified, trusted sources.

If Bill Gates, the founder of Microsoft, approached you tomorrow and said, "I'm looking to grow my company and I would like for you to invest $200." Would you do it? Or what if Phil Knight, the founder of Nike, wanted $200 from you to grow his company, would you invest your hard earned cash into these companies? I'm going to guess and say that you would because these are solid companies that have been around for years with proven track records of success. In order to raise funds, some businesses sell pieces of ownership of their companies known as shares or stocks. It's similar to the way your school's canteen breaks the pie of a pizza down and sells it by the slice. But instead of 8 slices, there could be thousands of slices available.

Think of the Stock Market as the place you can go to when you want to buy and sell shares of publicly-traded companies. Based on the value of these companies you choose to buy, the stock price will fluctuate and either rise or drop in stock price. As the company grows in value, so does your stock. But the opposite is also true: if your company drops in value, so does your stock. For example, you bought a share of XYZ Company for $100, and 6 months later this same stock is worth $130. Your money had a 30% return without you having to punch a time clock to make it. Remember that your money has to make money for you as well.

One of the biggest lies that kept me from buying stocks earlier was that I thought I needed a lot of money to start. But, the truth was that I could invest on my own individual financial level, meaning I could invest the amount that was comfortable for my finances to handle. Depending on your brokerage, stocks can be purchased on a fractional basis. For example, you want to own XYZ Company that is selling at $500 a share, but you only have $50 to invest. You can afford to buy

1/10th of a share. But over time, purchases like that could add up to a much bigger stock portfolio. I opened my daughter's first investment account with 0.05 cents. I'm sure you're able to find some loose change somewhere. Even if you have to *nickel and dime* your way to your first few shares, that's perfectly fine! The truth is that it doesn't take a lot of money to open your account and it doesn't take a lot to start buying shares. And if you are under 18 years old, you could have your parents select and open you up a custodial account with a brokerage.

A brokerage account is an account that gives you access to buy and sell shares. Think of it like you do a bank account but with the added bonus of being able to buy and sell your shares. There are plenty of brokerages to choose from, but select the one(s) that work best for you. When choosing between brokerages, ask yourself these question

How long has this company been in business?
What kind of fee's will they charge me for having my account(s) here?
What's the minimum amount I need to start and maintain my account(s)?
What are some reviews for their current customers?
Have they been involved in any illegal activities? and
Can I buy fractional shares?
You can check out bankrate.com to compare benefits and features of various brokerage accounts.

There are 2 time frames when it comes to owning stocks: there's short-term and long-term. Common short-term time frame stock ownership options are: day trading, swing trading, and options trading. Day trading is when you get in and out of your stock position on the same day. Swing trading is when you keep your stock position anywhere from days to months. Options trading is when you purchase contracts for the option of the ownership of stocks for a certain price and timeframe. The long-term time frame is when you plan on holding your stocks from years to forever. Obviously one of the main goals of owning stocks is the appreciation in price over the years. Another way to increase your wealth with long-term stock ownership are payouts known as *dividends*.

Dividends are your share of the profits that the company made over a certain timeframe, and being that the company used your money to help grow, this is your portion of the profits. It's important for you to know that not all companies pay out dividends, but the ones that do pay out dividends base the payouts on the amount of shares you own and when you purchased the stock. The timeframe of dividend payouts will vary by stock. Some people choose to receive that payment and others choose to have that payout purchase more stocks for them. Your goal should be to select companies that will grow your money. It's also important for you to know that you can make money when stock prices are dropping. This is known as shorting a stock. An example of shorting a stock is when you borrow and sell the stock of XYZ Company from your brokerage and then you would pay your brokerage back for that stock at a later time and lower price while keeping the difference.

Now, you might be thinking: "How do I know what stocks to pick?" That's a question that I can't answer, but it will always come back to your own research and your preferences. Think about stocks the same as you are partnering with a company to protect and grow your money. There are also some investors who have a preference of buying stocks in bulk rather than buying single stocks. Buying stocks in bulk could be similar to purchasing a variety pack of chips.

That one variety pack gets you multiple flavors of chips all in one package and, depending on what financial product you select, that one product could hold ownership of multiple companies. This could be done through investing in Index Funds, Mutual Funds, and/or ETFs.

For example, the very first stock I purchased for my son was a low-cost S&P 500 Index Fund. I paid $45 for 1 share, and that gave my son a small fraction of ownership in the top 500 companies on the market.

Exchange-Traded Funds or ETFs are a group of stocks that function as a single stock. Mutual Funds are monies that are pooled together from a certain group of people and managed by a professional. Index Investing is when you invest in a particular group of stocks. According to CNBC, "The average annualized total return for the S&P 500 index over the past 90 years is 9.8%. I haven't come across any bank that would pay me that kind of interest on any of their checking or savings accounts. This rate of return is one of the many benefits that attract people to this style of investing.

With an account that tracks an Index, your stock holdings are also diverse and not just tied to 1 particular sector. As previously mentioned, some brokerages also offer fractional share purchases with a low minimum buy in and charge low fees to own. In other words, it doesn't take a lot of money to start, maintain, and grow these accounts.

You can fund your stock account by making it a regular expense through your paycheck or bonus money if you're not working. Whether you're working part-time, full-time, or sometime, it's the consistent dollar that always adds up. You can do what's known as *Dollar Cost Average*. This is when you invest the same amount of money regardless if it's a bull or a bear market. Bull Market is when the market is rising and a Bear Market has dropped 20% or more. Some Investors are happy to buy good quality companies in a *Bear Market* because they view the stocks as being on sale.

Keep in mind, 3 common goals for stock ownership are: asset appreciation, dividend income, and compound interest. Appreciation is when the stock rises in value, so if you're holding for the long-term, bear markets are appealing to some investors because of the profit that could be made through the stock recovering. Dividend income is when you are getting your income from your share of the company's profits. Again, compound interest is when your interest from your money makes you even more money. Albert Einstein is quoted for saying; "Compound Interest is the 8th wonder of the world. Those who understand it, earn it; those who don't pay it."

A concept I wish I heard of when I was your age is the F.I.R.E. Movement. It stands for *Financial Independence Retire Early*. The concept is based on the notion that a financial number and not a person's age determines retirement. This is achieved by having a stock portfolio big enough that their dividend income exceeds all of their expenses. If you want to retire before you reach your 60s or 70s, start building towards it now as a teenager.

The financial dollar amount needed for your early retirement is known as your fire number. People who strive to achieve this number are very aggressive in building their portfolio. They live below their means and invest as much as possible into their stock portfolio. I know too many people who never got to experience truly living because of their money, and I know too many people who might not ever reach their goal of full-time retirement because of their money. And I don't want that for you. Make your full-time retirement an early and often financial priority for your money. In all your learning, educate yourself on how to create wealth in the stock market.

CHAPTER 8

EMPOWERMENT

Albert Einstein is quoted for saying the following: “Doing the same thing over and over and expecting different results is the definition of insanity.” The most important person responsible for improving your circumstances will always be you, so you can’t make the same mistakes as others around you and expect a better outcome. The quality of your life will be determined by the disciplined, consistent efforts you put into improving your circumstances. This is true when it comes to your money and also true when it comes to life in general. As a student, you don’t get much say over the physical environment in which you live and grow up, but as an adult, the environment you live in is a direct reflection of the decisions you make.

I want you to dream big and then make time everyday to work towards turning your dream into reality. Use your youth to your advantage of opportunities, start early, and stay consistent when you are in pursuit of your dreams. You might have to go on your journey to your personal greatness alone, and that’s okay. The majority of working adults are struggling financially, so it’s quite alright to be a loner when it comes to your financial empowerment. Every dollar you don’t have to borrow, every dollar you save, every stock you buy, and every dollar you budget can be used for your empowerment to avoid living paycheck-to-paycheck.

You now have information to build your financial foundation, so please don't let it go to waste. It might seem like you have a long road ahead of you, and depending on your circumstances you probably do. But ask yourself these questions:

What could your finances look like within the next 5-10 years if you go all in on building wealth?

Do you have parents that you would like to see retire and actually start experiencing

pleasures in life instead of always working? What if you could provide that opportunity for them?

Would you like to travel and see and experience different parts of the world?

What would it feel like to be able to afford a house in any neighborhood you desire?

What would it feel like to be able to own your dream car?

What would your life look like if you weren't at the mercy of a manager and a job that you dislike?

I haven't come across a student yet whose heart's desire was to struggle financially as an adult, but because of the decisions that some people make, paycheck-to-paycheck is exactly the lifestyle they enter into.

The only peer pressure you should tolerate is pressure that's challenging you to go harder for your dreams and goals. **Don't start bad habits by engaging with addictive activities as a student that you'll be fighting your entire adult life to break.** Don't smoke, drink, or sex your dreams into an early grave. Your future is much bigger than a quick moment of pleasure that you can spend the rest of your life paying for. Avoid negative people and influences at all costs. So many people have no goals and dreams of their own, so they spend the majority of their time chilling. Don't let that be you. As you're in the process of building your dream life, don't allow for too much idle time. No one is going to cut a check to give you your dreams: you are going to have to go pay for them. Budget your income, avoid debt, build and maintain good credit, stack your cash, and buy assets. These should be priorities when it comes to your money.

I hope I've informed and inspired you to pursue the kind of money you want and not settle for what you were given. Don't let procrastination delay your dreams. Remember, the small, consistent dollar always adds up.

Made in the USA
Columbia, SC
06 March 2024

32297199R00043